Alfred's Premier Piano

MW00803309

Dennis Alexander • Gayle Kowalchyk • E. L. Lancaster • Victoria McArthur • Martha Mier

Alfred's *Premier Piano Course* Performance Book 6 includes motivational music in a variety of styles, reinforcing concepts introduced in the Lesson Book 6.

The pieces in this book correlate page by page with the materials in Lesson Book 6. They should be assigned according to the instructions in the upper right corner of each page of this book. They also may be assigned as review material at any time after the student has passed the designated Lesson Book page.

Downloadable MP3 files of audio performances on acoustic piano as well as orchestrated accompaniments are available. For more information, see page 40.

Performance skills and musical understanding are enhanced through *Premier Performer* suggestions. Students will enjoy performing these pieces for family and friends in a formal recital or on special occasions. See the List of Compositions on page 40.

All music selections composed or arranged by Dennis Alexander and Martha Mier.

Edited by Morton Manus

Cover Design by Ted Engelbart
Interior Design by Tom Gerou
Illustrations by Jimmy Holder
Music Engraving by Linda Lusk

ISBN-10: 0-7390-6892-X
ISBN-13: 978-0-7390-6892-2

Use with Alfred's Premier Piano Course,
Lesson Book 6, pages 2–3

Twelve O'Clock Jump

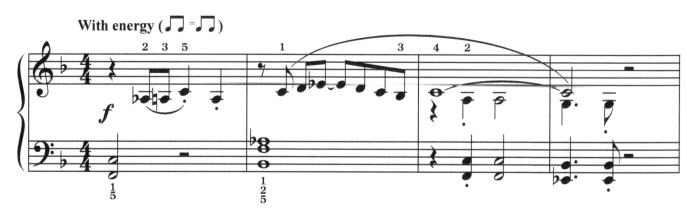

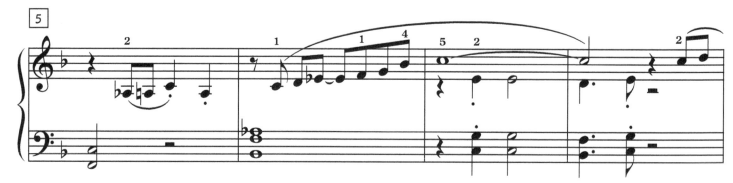

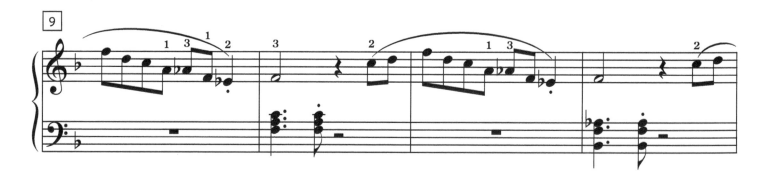

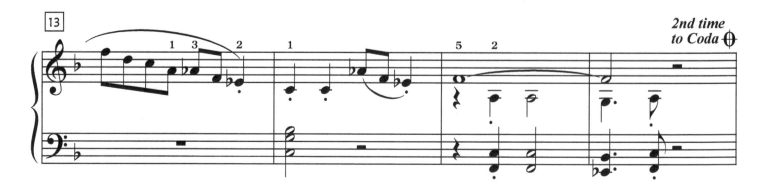

Lesson Book: pages 4–5

Cossack Dance

🔊 2

Premier Performer *Play the opening section boldly. Beginning in measure 17, use a gentler, legato touch.*

Serenade de Seville*

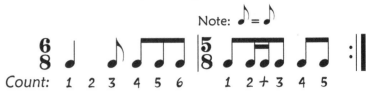

Rhythm Workout

On your lap, tap the rhythm 3 times daily as you count aloud. Keep the eighth notes equal.

🔊 3

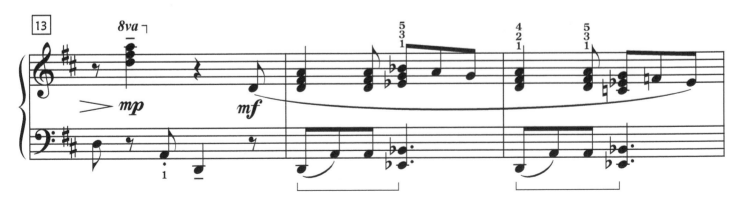

* Seville is a city in southern Spain known for its art and literature.

Rhythm Workout

On your lap, tap the rhythm 3 times daily
as you count aloud.

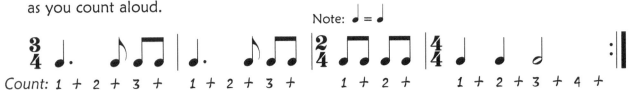

Count: 1 + 2 + 3 +   1 + 2 + 3 +   1 + 2 +   1 + 2 + 3 + 4 +

In the Village
(For Children, Volume 1)

 4

Béla Bartók
(1881–1945)

Con moto *(with motion)*

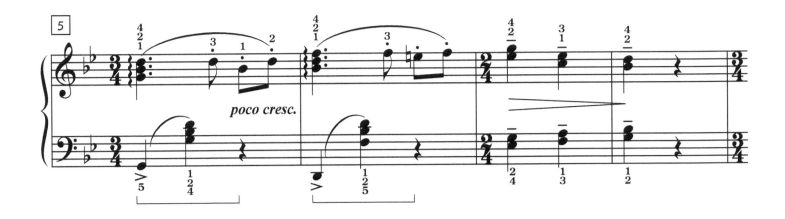

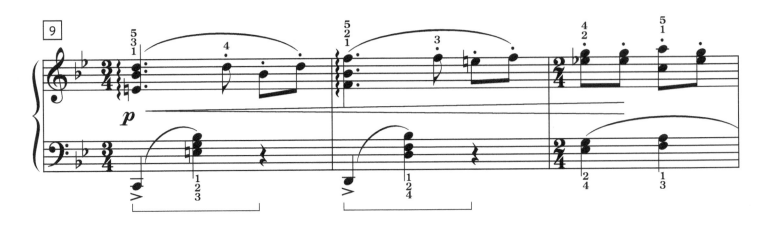

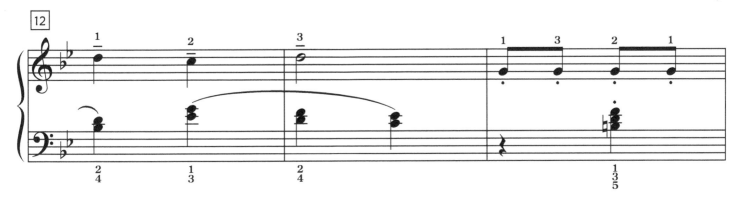

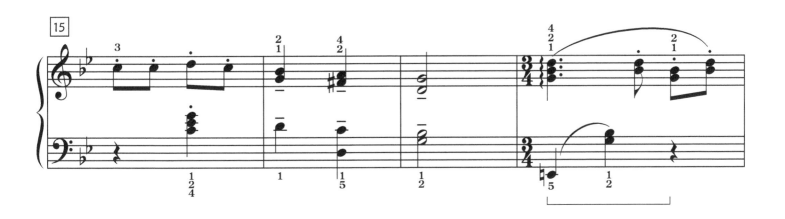

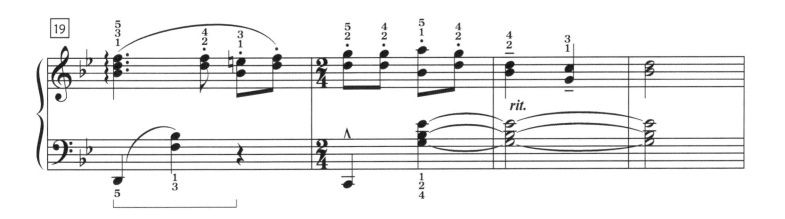

Premier Performer

Maintain a steady tempo throughout by keeping the quarter notes in 2/4 time equal to the quarter notes in 3/4 time.

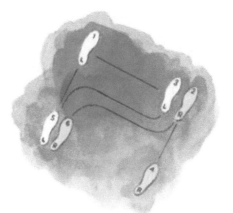

Waltz in B Minor

🔊 5

Cornelius Gurlitt (1820–1901)
Op. 205, No. 10

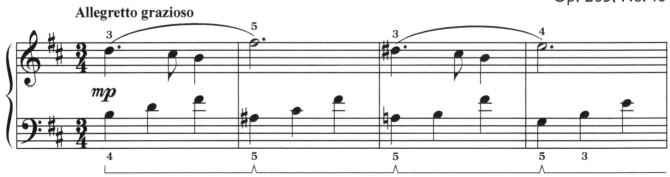

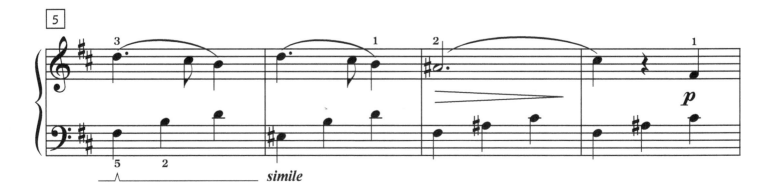

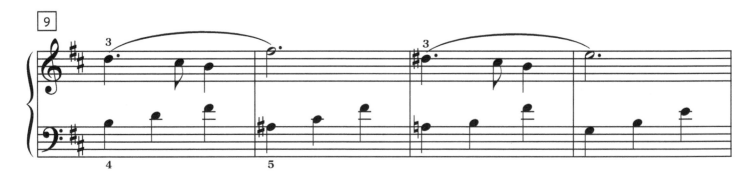

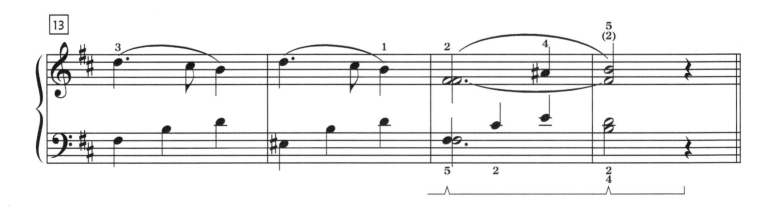

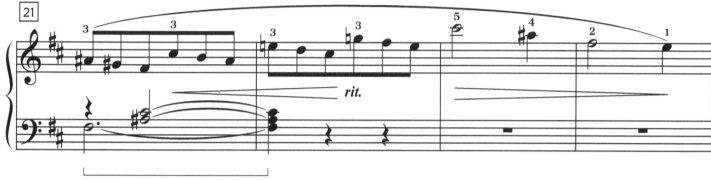

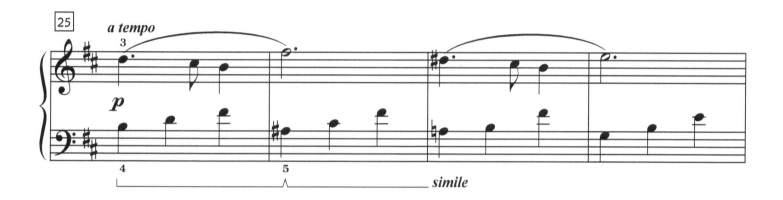

Premier Performer

In measures 15–16 and 31–32, hold the F♯ in treble clef for 5 full beats and the F♯ in bass clef for 3 full beats.

Friday Night Rock

Solfeggio* in C Minor

Carl Philipp Emanuel Bach
(1714–1788)

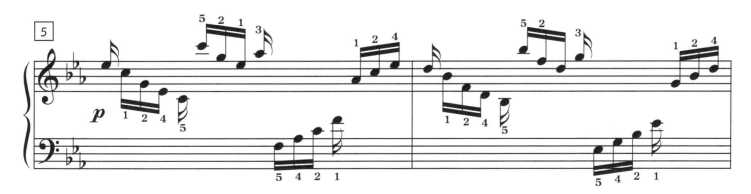

* A *solfeggio* is a vocal exercise sung with syllables (do, re, mi, etc.) for the notes.

Lesson Book: page 18

Trevi Fountain*

🔊 8

Moderately, with expression

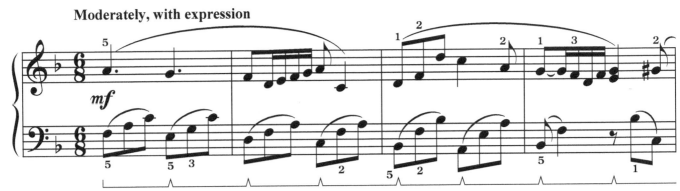

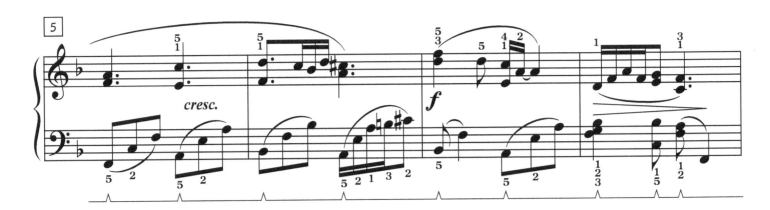

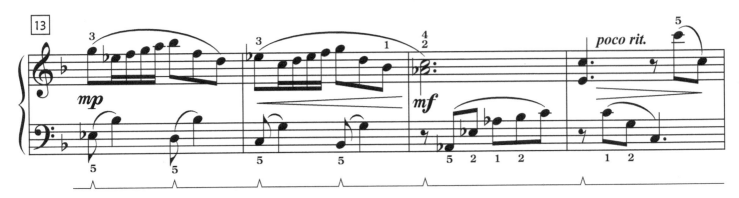

* The Trevi Fountain, completed in 1762, is located in Rome, Italy. According to one legend,
visitors who throw a coin in the fountain will return to the city someday.

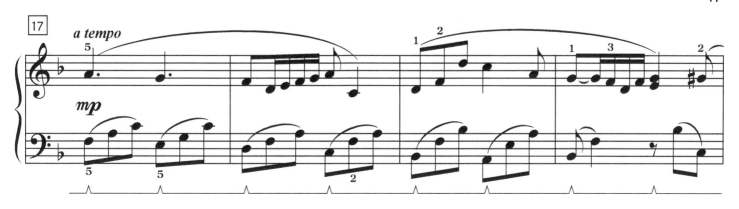

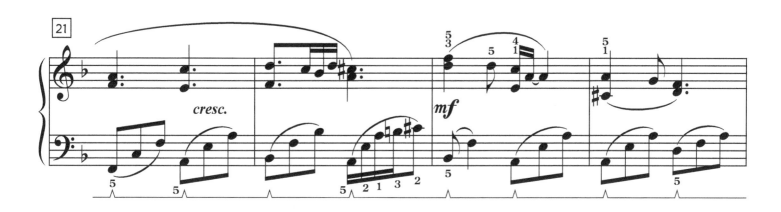

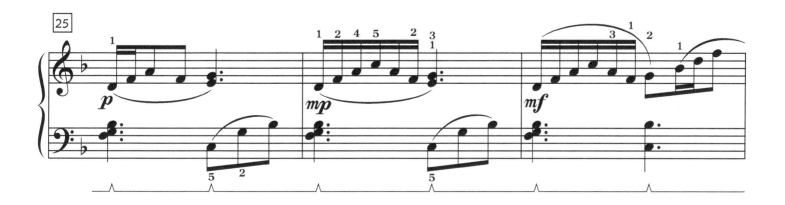

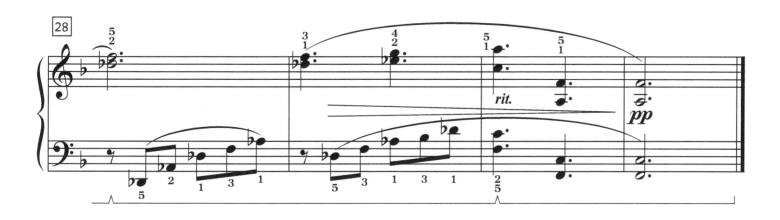

Premier Performer *Listen for beautiful singing lines in the RH melody and keep the LH softer throughout.*

The Wild Rider
(Album for the Young)

🔊 9

Robert Schumann (1810–1856)
Op. 68, No. 8

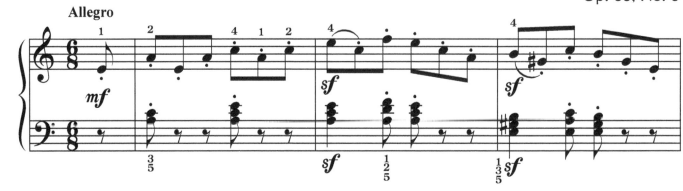

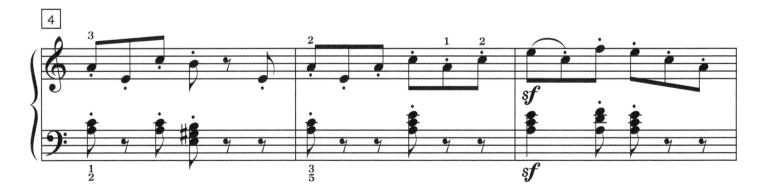

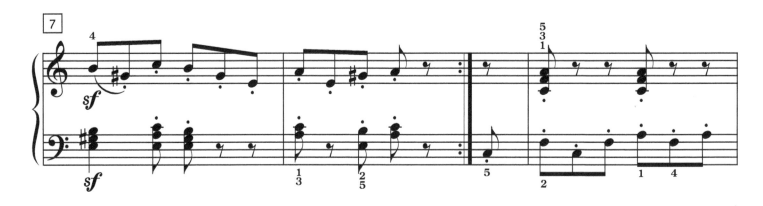

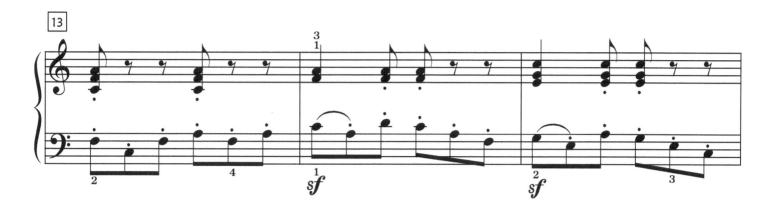

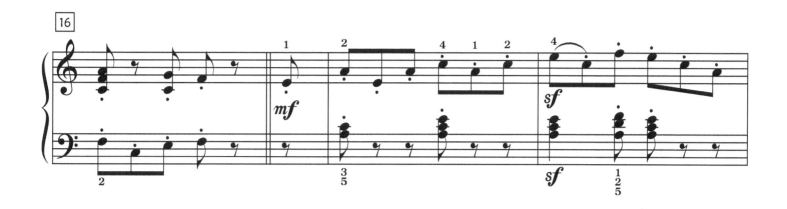

Premier Performer *Bring out the two-note slurs in* The Wild Rider *by playing the notes marked* **sf** *with a strong accent.*

Southern Dreams

 10

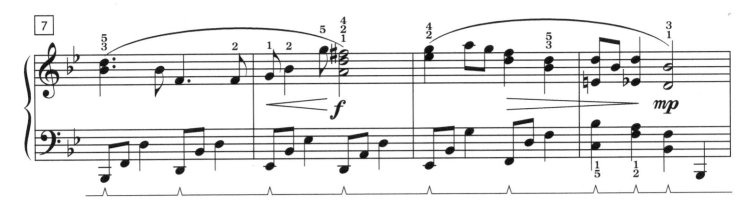

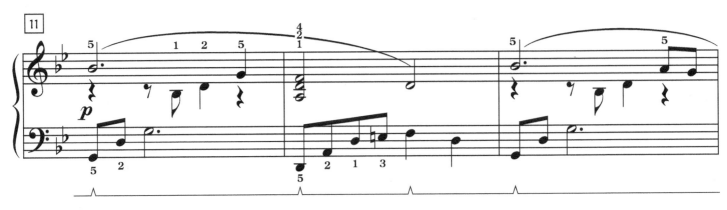

Lesson Book: page 28

Valse mystérieuse

🔊 11

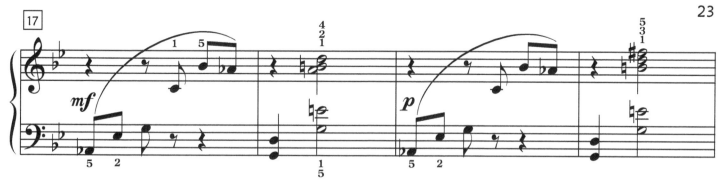

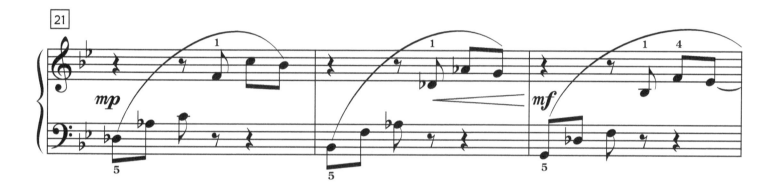

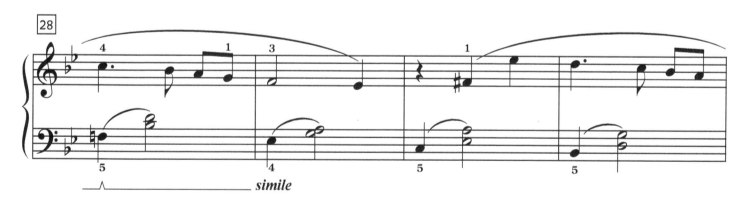

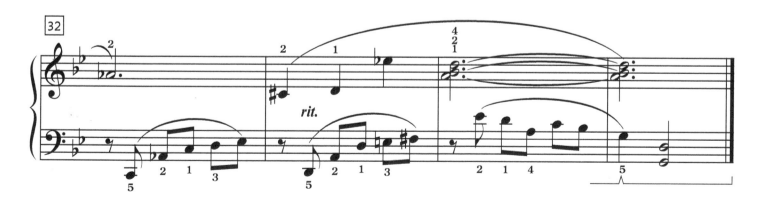

The Avalanche

🔊 12

Stephen Heller (1813–1888)
Op. 45, No. 2

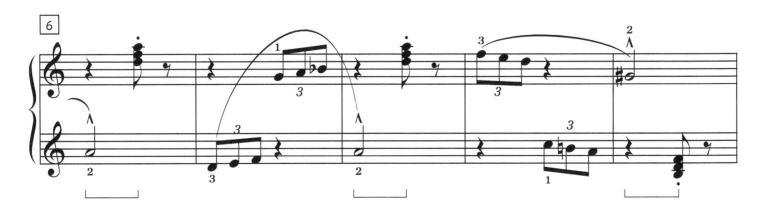

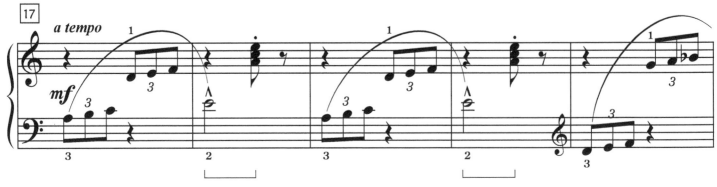

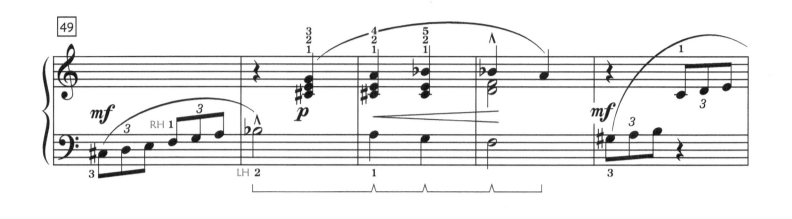

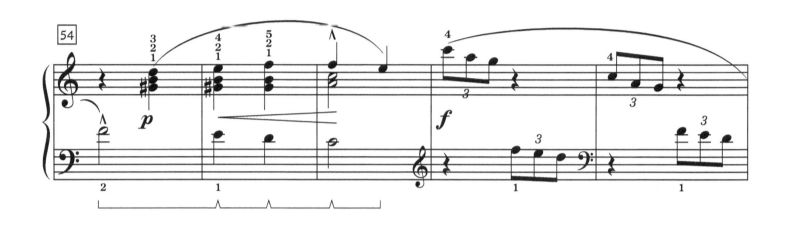

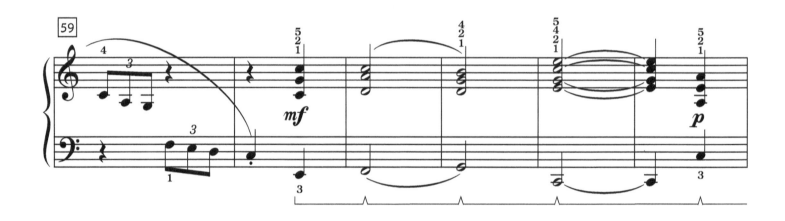

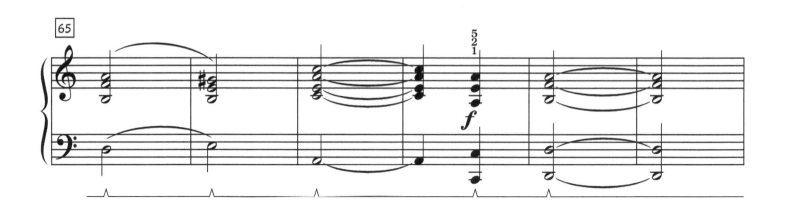

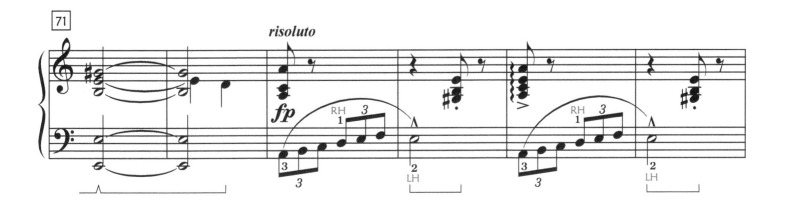

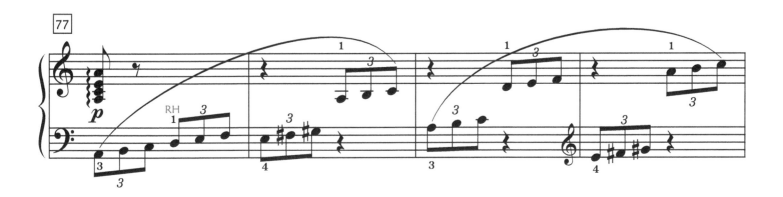

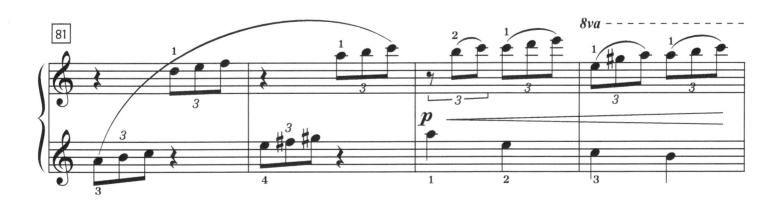

![star] **Premier Performer**
Maintain firm fingertips and a rounded hand position to smoothly connect the triplets as they move from hand to hand.

1950s Rock 'n' Roll

🔊 **13**

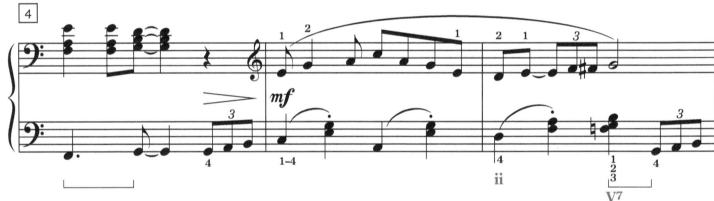

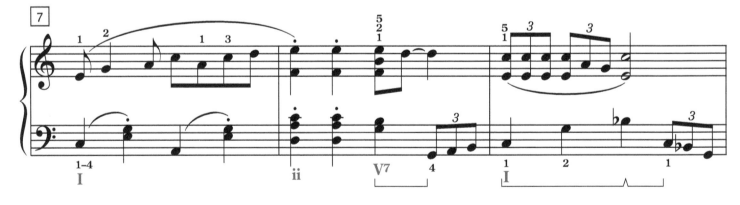

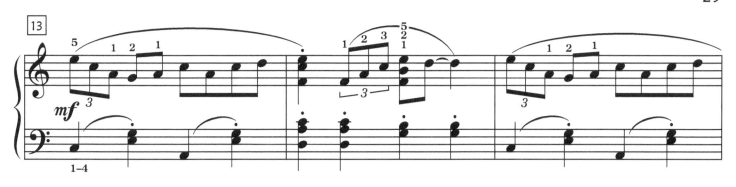

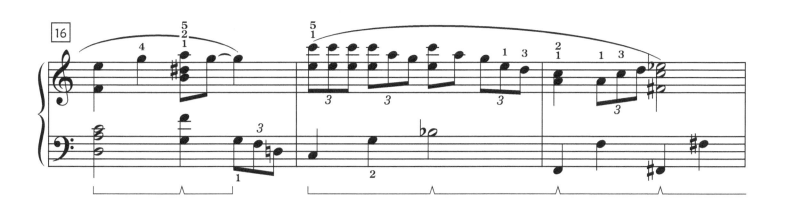

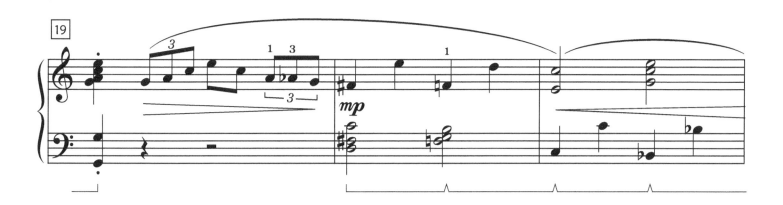

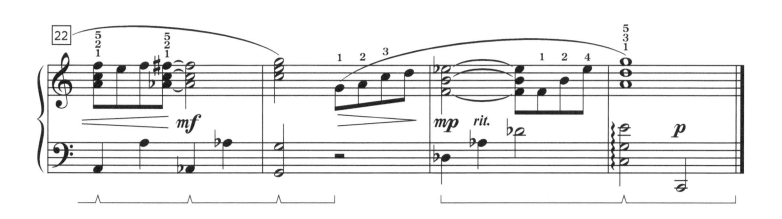

Premier Performer   *Play the ♪♪ with swing, but play ♪♪♪ evenly.*

Jazz Reflections

 14

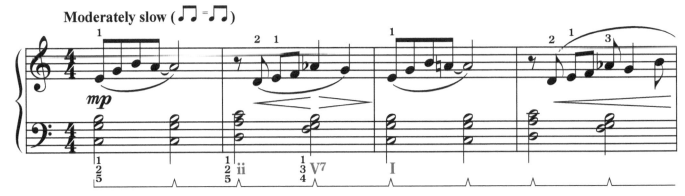

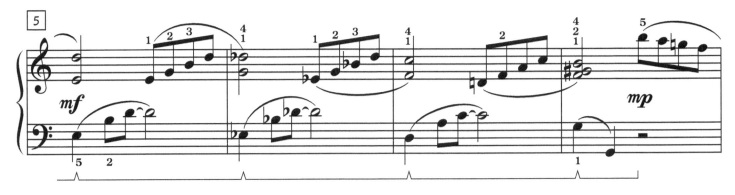

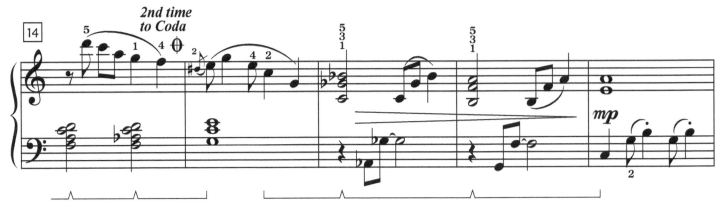

Sonatina in G Major

🔊 15

Ludwig van Beethoven
(1770–1827)

Moderato

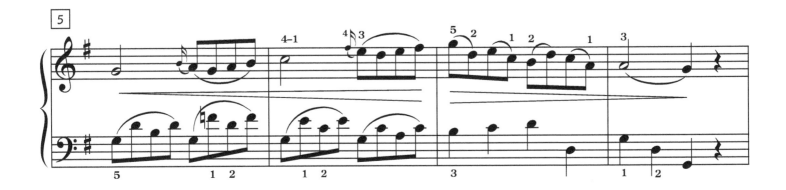

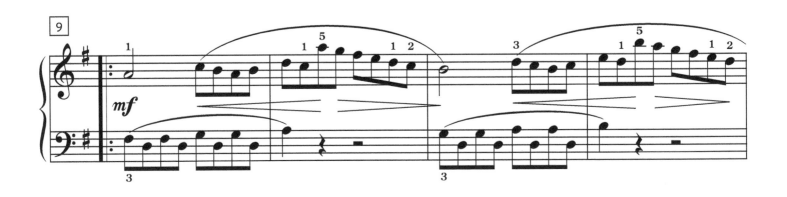

*Alternate:

🔊 16

ROMANZE
Allegretto

Reverie

Lesson Book: pages 48–49

🔊 17

Premier Performer *Perform Sicilienne (Lesson Book 6, pp. 48–49) followed immediately by Reverie to create a longer piece.*

Magnolia Rag

🔊 **18**

List of Compositions

*MP3 files of audio performances on acoustic piano and orchestrated accompaniments are available for download at **alfred.com/ppcperformance**. There are four versions of each piece:*

*1. A digitally orchestrated accompaniment **with** piano.*

*2. A digitally orchestrated accompaniment **without** piano.*

*3. A **practice tempo** performed on acoustic piano.*

*4. A **performance tempo** performed on acoustic piano.*

TNT 2 Custom Mix Software, also available for download at the link listed above, allows the user to change tempos in these audio files. In addition, General MIDI files are available for download. These recordings add musical interest and motivate students in the lesson and during practice.

<table>
<tr><td></td><td>**Track**</td><td>**Page**</td></tr>
<tr><td>1950s Rock 'n' Roll</td><td>13</td><td>28</td></tr>
<tr><td>Avalanche, The</td><td>12</td><td>24</td></tr>
<tr><td>Cossack Dance</td><td>2</td><td>4</td></tr>
<tr><td>Friday Night Rock</td><td>6</td><td>12</td></tr>
<tr><td>In the Village</td><td>4</td><td>8</td></tr>
<tr><td>Jazz Reflections</td><td>14</td><td>30</td></tr>
<tr><td>Magnolia Rag</td><td>18</td><td>38</td></tr>
<tr><td>Reverie</td><td>17</td><td>36</td></tr>
<tr><td>Serenade de Seville</td><td>3</td><td>6</td></tr>
<tr><td>Solfeggio in C Minor</td><td>7</td><td>13</td></tr>
<tr><td>Sonatina in G Major</td><td></td><td></td></tr>
<tr><td>   First Movement</td><td>15</td><td>32</td></tr>
<tr><td>   Second Movement</td><td>16</td><td>34</td></tr>
<tr><td>Southern Dreams</td><td>10</td><td>20</td></tr>
<tr><td>Trevi Fountain</td><td>8</td><td>16</td></tr>
<tr><td>Twelve O'Clock Jump</td><td>1</td><td>2</td></tr>
<tr><td>Valse mystérieuse</td><td>11</td><td>22</td></tr>
<tr><td>Waltz in B Minor</td><td>5</td><td>10</td></tr>
<tr><td>Wild Rider, The</td><td>9</td><td>18</td></tr>
</table>

TNT 2 Software Instructions

To install the **TNT 2** software, double-click on the installer file. Once it is installed, you will be able to slow down or speed up each MP3, loop playback, and select specific sections for practicing.

TNT 2 System Requirements:

Windows
10, 8, 7, Vista, XP
QuickTime 7.6.7 or higher
1.8 GHz processor or faster
340 MB hard drive space, 2 GB RAM minimum
Speakers or headphones
Internet access required for updates

Macintosh
OS X 10.4 or higher (Intel only)
QuickTime 7.6.7 or higher
450 MB hard drive space, 2 GB RAM minimum
Speakers or headphones
Internet access for updates

Performances by Scott Price